My State
IDAHO

By Christina Earley

TABLE OF CONTENTS

A Crabtree Seedlings Book

Crabtree Publishing
crabtreebooks.com

School-to-Home Support for Caregivers and Teachers

This book helps children grow by letting them practice reading. Here are a few guiding questions to help the reader build his or her comprehension skills. Possible answers appear in red.

Before Reading:

- What do I know about Idaho?
    - *I know that Idaho is a state.*
    - *I know that Idaho grows a lot of potatoes.*

- What do I want to learn about Idaho?
    - *I want to learn which famous people were born in Idaho.*
    - *I want to learn what the state flag looks like.*

During Reading:

- What have I learned so far?
    - *I have learned that Boise is the state capital of Idaho.*
    - *I have learned that the tallest sand dune in North America is in Bruneau Dunes State Park.*

- I wonder why...
    - *I wonder why the state flower is the Syringa.*
    - *I wonder why Idaho produces almost one-third of the potatoes in the U.S.*

After Reading:

- What did I learn about Idaho?
    - *I have learned that I can ride in a paddleboat at Julia Davis Park.*
    - *I have learned that the state insect is the monarch butterfly.*

- Read the book again and look for the glossary words.
    - *I see the word **capital** on page 6, and the word **dunes** on page 14. The other glossary words are found on pages 22 and 23.*

IDAHO
Hi! My name is Liam.
Welcome to Idaho!

I live in Priest River. My family lives on a farm.

Priest River was first **settled** in 1889!

Idaho is in the northwestern United States. The **capital** is Boise.

Fun Fact: Boise is the largest city in Idaho.

The monarch butterfly is the state insect.

The Syringa is the state flower.

We grow a lot of potatoes. Some of them are used to make french fries.

Fun Fact: Idaho **produces** almost one-third of the potatoes in the U.S.

My state flag is dark blue. The state **seal** is in the middle.

I love watching the minor league Idaho Steelheads play ice hockey.

I like to visit Bruneau **Dunes** State Park. Sometimes I go horseback riding.

Fun Fact: The tallest sand dune in North America is found here.

I enjoy fishing on the Saint Joe River.

Shoshone Falls is beautiful. The waterfall is higher than Niagara Falls!

Astronaut James F. Reilly was born in Idaho. Olympic skier Picabo Street was also born in Idaho.

Fun Fact: Interpreter and guide Sacagawea was born in the Salmon River region of Idaho.

I love riding in a **paddleboat** at Julia Davis Park.

I enjoy going to Zoo Boise with my family.

Glossary

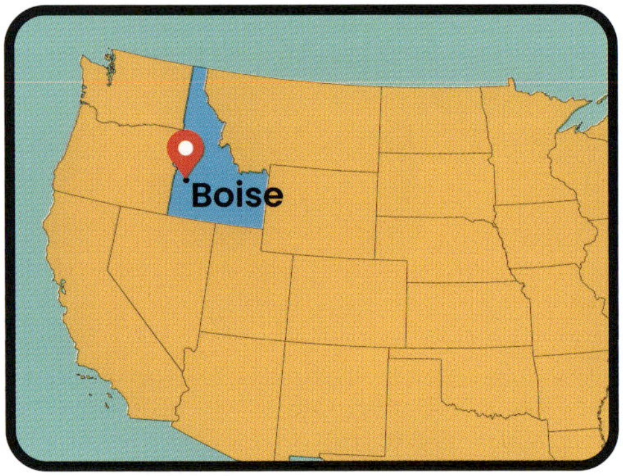

capital (cap-ih-tuhl): The city or town where the government of a country, state, or province is located

dunes (dewnz): Hills of sand formed by the wind

paddleboat (pad-uhl-boht): A small boat with paddle wheels that are turned by pedals

produces (pruh-doos-es): Makes or grows something for sale or use

seal (seel): A special design that is used on important papers and other items

settled (set-ld): To have people move to a place and make it their home

Index

About the Author

Christina Earley lives in sunny South Florida with her husband and son. She enjoys traveling around the United States and learning about different historical places. Her hobbies include hiking, yoga, and baking.

Written by: Christina Earley
Designed and Illustrated by: Bobbie Houser
Series Development: James Earley
Proofreader: Melissa Boyce
Educational Consultant: Marie Lemke M.Ed.

Photographs:
Alamy: ZUMA: p. 13; dpa picture alliance: p. 18 right; ZUMA Press: p. 19; David R. Frazier Photolibrary, Inc.: p. 20, 22
NASA: p. 18 left
Shutterstock: CSNafzger: cover; Gregory Johnston: p. 3; Kirk Fisher: p. 4-5, 23; Volina: p. 6, 22; Charles Knowles: p. 7; CHAINFOTO24: p. 8; nnattalli: p. 9; Steve Photography: p. 10-11; New Africa: p. 11, 23; Millenius: p. 12, 23; Sam Strickler: p. 14; Peter Milota Jr: p. 14-15, 22; OLya_L: p. 16; Png Studio Photography: p. 17; Robert Crow: p. 21

Crabtree Publishing

crabtreebooks.com 800-387-7650

Printed in the U.S.A./012023/CG20220815

Published in Canada
Crabtree Publishing
616 Welland Avenue
St. Catharines, Ontario
L2M 5V6

Published in the United States
Crabtree Publishing
347 Fifth Avenue
Suite 1402-145
New York, New York, 10016

Library and Archives Canada Cataloguing in Publication
Available at Library and Archives Canada

Library of Congress Cataloging-in-Publication Data
Available at the Library of Congress

Hardcover: 978-1-0398-0246-9
Paperback: 978-1-0398-0256-8
Ebook (pdf): 978-1-0398-0276-6
Epub: 978-1-0398-0266-7